DRAGONFLIES AFGHAN

INTERMEDIATE
Shown on Front Cover.

Finished Size: 45" x 63" (114.5 cm x 160 cm)

MATERIALS
Medium/Worsted Weight Yarn 〔4〕
   [5 ounces, 278 yards
   (141 grams, 254 meters) per skein]:
      Variegated - 5 skeins
   [7 ounces, 364 yards
   (198 grams, 333 meters) per skein]:
      Blue - 2 skeins
      Green - 2 skeins
      Black - 1 skein
      White - 1 skein
Crochet hook, size H (5 mm) **or** size needed for gauge
Yarn needle

GAUGE: Block A = 9"w x 12"h
   (22.75 cm x 30.5 cm);
   Block B = 12" (30.5 cm) square
   14 dc = 4" (10 cm)

Gauge Swatch: 5¼"w x 9¼"h
   (13.25 cm x 23.5 cm)
Work same as Block A through Rnd 5.

BLOCK A (Make 10)
With Black, ch 17.

Rnd 1 (Right side): (Dc, ch 2, slip st) in fourth ch from hook **(3 skipped chs count as first dc)**, sc in next 5 chs, slip st in last 8 chs, ch 1; working in free loops on opposite side of beginning ch *(Fig. 5b, page 17)*, slip st in first 8 chs, sc in next 5 chs, slip st in next ch, ch 2; join with slip st to first dc, finish off.

Note: Loop a short piece of yarn around any stitch to mark Rnd 1 as **right** side.

Rnd 2: With **right** side facing and working in Back Loops Only *(Fig. 4, page 17)*, skip same st as joining and join Blue with dc in next dc *(see Joining With Dc, page 17)*; (2 dc, ch 2, 2 dc) in next ch, dc in next ch, working **around** next slip st *(Fig. 6, page 17)*, dc in beginning ch, working in Back Loops Only, dc in next 5 sc, place marker in Front Loop Only of last sc worked into for Wing placement, dc in next 10 sts, (2 dc, ch 2, 2 dc) in next slip st, dc in next ch, (2 dc, ch 2, 2 dc) in next slip st, dc in next 9 sts, place marker in Front Loop Only of last sc worked into for Wing placement, dc in next 5 sc, working **around** next slip st, dc in beginning ch, working in Back Loops Only, dc in next ch, (2 dc, ch 2, 2 dc) in next ch; join with slip st to **both** loops of first dc: 46 dc and 4 ch-2 sps.

Rnd 3: Ch 3 **(counts as first dc, now and throughout)**, working in both loops, dc in next 2 dc, (2 dc, ch 2, 2 dc) in next ch-2 sp, dc in next 18 dc, (2 dc, ch 2, 2 dc) in next ch-2 sp, dc in next 5 dc, (2 dc, ch 2, 2 dc) in next ch-2 sp, dc in next 18 dc, (2 dc, ch 2, 2 dc) in next ch-2 sp, dc in last 2 dc; join with slip st to first dc: 62 dc and 4 ch-2 sps.

Rnds 4 and 5: Ch 3, dc in next dc and in each dc around working (2 dc, ch 2, 2 dc) in each corner ch-2 sp; join with slip st to first dc: 94 dc and 4 ch-2 sps.

Finish off.

Rnd 6: With **right** side facing, join Green with dc in first corner ch-2 sp; (dc, ch 2, 2 dc) in same sp, ch 2, † skip next 2 dc, (dc in next 2 dc, ch 2, skip next 2 dc) across to next corner ch-2 sp, (2 dc, ch 2) twice in corner ch-2 sp, (skip next 2 dc, dc in next 2 dc, ch 2) 4 times, skip next dc †, (2 dc, ch 2) twice in next corner ch-2 sp, repeat from † to † once; join with slip st to first dc, finish off: 60 dc and 30 ch-2 sps.

Instructions continued on page 3.

Rnd 7: With **right** side facing, join Variegated with dc in third corner ch-2 sp; (2 dc, ch 2, 3 dc) in same sp, 3 dc in next ch-2 sp and in each ch-2 sp around working (3 dc, ch 2, 3 dc) in each corner ch-2 sp; join with slip st to first dc: 102 dc and 4 ch-2 sps.

Rnd 8: Slip st in next 2 dc and in next ch-2 sp, ch 3, (2 dc, ch 2, 3 dc) in same sp, skip next 3 dc, [3 dc in sp **before** next dc *(Fig. 7, page 17)*, skip next 3 dc] across to next corner ch-2 sp, ★ (3 dc, ch 2, 3 dc) in corner ch-3 sp, skip next 3 dc, (3 dc, in sp **before** next dc, skip next 3 dc) across to next corner ch-2 sp; repeat from ★ 2 times **more**; join with slip st to first dc, finish off: 114 dc and 4 ch-2 sps.

First Pair of Wings: With **right** side facing and working in free loops of sc on Rnd 1 *(Fig. 5a, page 17)*, join White with slip st in first marked sc; remove marker, ch 8, slip st into side of twelfth dc **after** corner ch-2 sp on Rnd 5 *(Fig. 1)*, sc in second ch from hook and in each ch across, slip st in free loop of next sc on Rnd 1, ch 6, slip st into side of twelfth dc **after** corner ch-2 sp on Rnd 4, sc in second ch from hook and in each ch across, slip st in free loop of next sc on Rnd 1; finish off.

Fig. 1

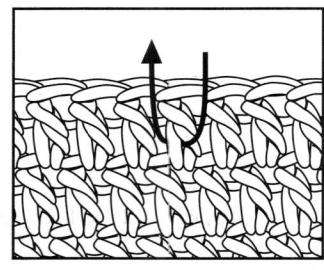

Second Pair of Wings: With **right** side facing and working in free loops of sc on Rnd 1, join White with slip st in second marked sc; remove marker, ch 6, slip st into side of eleventh dc **before** next corner ch-2 sp on Rnd 4, sc in second ch from hook and in each ch across, slip st in free loop of next sc on Rnd 1, ch 8, slip st into side of eleventh dc **before** next corner ch-2 sp on Rnd 5, sc in second ch from hook and in each ch across, slip st in free loop of next sc on Rnd 1; finish off.

BLOCK B (Make 10)

With Black, ch 17.

Rnd 1: Work same as Block A, page 2.

Rnds 2-5: With Green, work same as Block A.

Finish off.

Rnd 6: With Blue, work same as Block A.

Rnds 7 and 8: Work same as Block A; at end of Rnd 8, do **not** finish off.

Begin working in rows.

Row 1: Slip st in next 2 dc and in next ch-2 sp, ch 3, 2 dc in same sp, skip next 3 dc, (3 dc in sp **before** next dc, skip next 3 dc) across to next corner ch-2 sp, 3 dc in corner ch-2 sp, leave remaining sts unworked: 36 dc.

Row 2: Ch 4 **(counts as first dc plus ch 1)**, turn; skip next 2 dc, 3 dc in sp **before** next dc, (skip next 3 dc, 3 dc in sp **before** next dc) across to last 3 dc, ch 1, skip next 2 dc, dc in last dc: 35 dc.

Row 3: Ch 3, turn; 2 dc in first ch-1 sp, skip next 3 dc, (3 dc in sp **before** next dc, skip next 3 dc) across to last ch-1 sp, 2 dc in last ch-1 sp, dc in last dc: 36 dc.

Rows 4 and 5: Repeat Rows 2 and 3.

Finish off.

Wings: Work same as Block A.

ASSEMBLY

Using Placement Diagram as a guide and Variegated, whipstitch Blocks together *(Fig. 8, page 17)*, forming 5 horizontal strips of 4 Blocks each; then whipstitch strips together in same manner.

PLACEMENT DIAGRAM

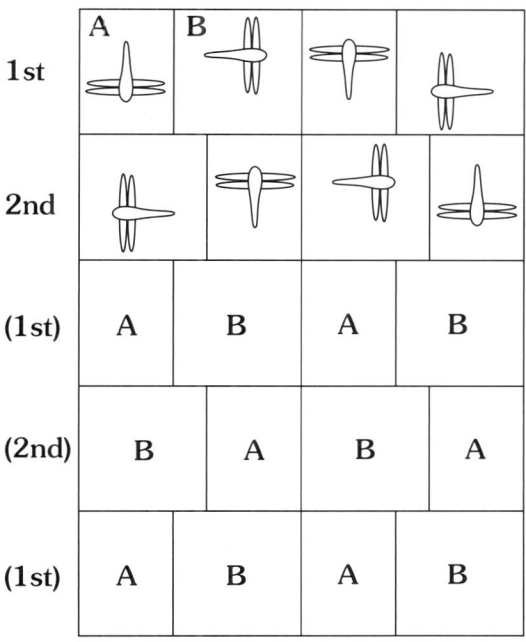

BORDER

Rnd 1: With **right** side facing and working across top edge, join Blue with dc in corner dc on Block B; (dc, ch 2, 2 dc) in same st, ch 2, skip next 2 dc, ♥ 2 dc in sp **before** next dc, (ch 2, skip next 3 dc, 2 dc in sp **before** next dc) 10 times, ch 2, skip next 3 dc, dc in next seam and in next sp, ch 2, (skip next 3 dc, 2 dc in sp **before** next dc, ch 2) 7 times, skip next 3 dc, dc in next sp, skip next seam, dc in next sp, ch 2, (skip next 3 dc, 2 dc in sp **before** next dc, ch 2) 10 times, skip next 3 dc ♥, dc in next sp, skip next seam, dc in next sp, ch 2, (skip next 3 dc, 2 dc in sp **before** next dc, ch 2) 7 times, skip next 3 dc, (2 dc, ch 2) twice in next corner ch-2 sp, (skip next 3 dc, 2 dc in sp **before** next dc, ch 2) 10 times, skip next 3 dc, † dc in next sp and in next seam; ch 2, working in end of rows across Block B, (skip next row, 2 dc in next row, ch 2) twice, skip last row, 2 dc in next sp, ch 2, (skip next 3 dc, 2 dc in sp **before** next dc, ch 2) 7 times, skip next 3 dc, dc in next sp, skip next seam, dc in next sp, ch 2, (skip next 3 dc, 2 dc in sp **before** next dc, ch 2) 10 times, skip next 3 dc †, repeat from † to † once, (2 dc, ch 2) twice in next corner ch-2 sp, (skip next 3 dc, 2 dc in sp **before** next dc, ch 2) 7 times, skip next 3 dc, dc in next sp and in next seam, ch 2, skip next 3 dc, repeat from ♥ to ♥ once; (2 dc, ch 2) twice in next corner ch-2 sp, (skip next 3 dc, 2 dc in sp **before** next dc, ch 2) 7 times, skip next 3 dc, 2 dc in next sp, ch 2, working in end of rows across Block B, (skip next row, 2 dc in next row, ch 2) twice, skip last row, ★ dc in next seam and in next sp, ch 2, (skip next 3 dc, 2 dc in sp **before** next dc, ch 2) 10 times, skip next 3 dc, dc in next sp, skip next seam, dc in next sp, ch 2, (skip next 3 dc, 2 dc in sp **before** next dc, ch 2) 7 times, skip next 3 dc, 2 dc in next sp, ch 2, working in end of rows across Block B, (skip next row, 2 dc in next row, ch 2) twice, skip last row; repeat from ★ once **more**; join with slip st to first dc, finish off: 192 ch-2 sps.

Rnd 2: With **right** side facing, join Green with dc in any corner ch-2 sp; (dc, ch 2, 2 dc) in same sp, ch 2, (2 dc in next ch-2 sp, ch 2) across to next corner ch-2 sp, ★ (2 dc, ch 2) twice in corner ch-2 sp, (2 dc in next ch-2 sp, ch 2) across to next corner ch-2 sp; repeat from ★ 2 times **more**; join with slip st to first dc, finish off.

Rnd 3: With **right** side facing, join Variegated with dc in any corner ch-2 sp; (2 dc, ch 2, 3 dc) in same sp, skip next dc, sc in sp **before** next dc, ★ † skip next ch-2 sp and next dc, (3 dc, ch 2, 3 dc) in sp **before** next dc, skip next ch-2 sp and next dc, sc in sp **before** next dc †; repeat from † to † across to next corner ch-2 sp, (3 dc, ch 2, 3 dc) in corner ch-2 sp; repeat from ★ 2 times **more**, then repeat from † to † across; join with slip st to first dc, finish off.

LADY BUGS AFGHAN

■■■□ INTERMEDIATE

Finished Size: 43½" x 60" (110.5 cm x 152.5 cm)

MATERIALS
Medium/Worsted Weight Yarn 🔵4🔵
  [6 ounces, 326 yards
  (170 grams, 298 meters) per skein]:
    White - 5 skeins
    Red - 1 skein
    Black - 1 skein
  [5 ounces, 302 yards
  (140 grams, 276 meters) per skein]:
    Green - 1 skein
Crochet hook, size H (5 mm) **or** size needed for gauge
Yarn needle

GAUGE: Block A = 9"w x 11½"h
  (22.75 cm x 29.25 cm);
  Block B = 11½" (29.25 cm) square
  13 dc = 4" (10 cm)

Gauge Swatch: 6¼"w x 8¼"h
  (16 cm x 21 cm)
Work same as Block A through Background Rnd 2.

STITCH GUIDE

TREBLE CROCHET *(abbreviated tr)*
YO twice, insert hook in st indicated, YO and pull up a loop (4 loops on hook), (YO and draw through 2 loops on hook) 3 times.

TR CLUSTER *(uses one sp)*
★ YO twice, insert hook in sp indicated, YO and pull up a loop, (YO and draw through 2 loops on hook) twice; repeat from ★ 2 times **more**, YO and draw through all 4 loops on hook.

2-DTR CLUSTER (uses one sp)
★ YO 3 times, insert hook in sp indicated, YO and pull up a loop, (YO and draw through 2 loops on hook) 3 times; repeat from ★ once **more**, YO and draw through all 3 loops on hook.

3-DTR CLUSTER (uses one sp)
★ YO 3 times, insert hook in sp indicated, YO and pull up a loop, (YO and draw through 2 loops on hook) 3 times; repeat from ★ 2 times **more**, YO and draw through all 4 loops on hook.

PICOT
Ch 3, slip st in third ch from hook.

BLOCK A (Make 10)
LADY BUG BODY
With Black, ch 13.

Rnd 1 (Right side)**:** Slip st in second ch from hook and in each ch across; working free loops on opposite side of beginning ch *(Fig. 5b, page 17)*, slip st in first 12 chs; join with slip st to Back Loop Only of first slip st *(Fig. 4, page 17)*: 24 slip sts.

Note: Loop a short piece of yarn around any stitch to mark Rnd 1 as **right** side.

Rnd 2: Ch 3 **(counts as first dc, now and throughout)**, working in Back Loops Only, dc in same st, 2 dc in next slip st, tr in next 9 slip sts, 2 dc in each of next 3 slip sts, tr in next 9 slip sts, 2 dc in next slip st; join with slip st to both loops of first dc: 30 sts.

Rnd 3: Ch 3, dc in same st, working in both loops, 2 dc in each of next 3 dc, tr in next 9 tr, 2 dc in each of next 6 dc, tr in next 9 tr, 2 dc in each of last 2 dc; join with slip st to first dc, finish off: 42 sts.

Instructions continued on page 7.

FIRST WING
Row 1: With **right** side facing and working in free loops of slip sts on Rnd 1 **(Fig. 5a, page 17)**, skip first slip st and join Red with dc in next slip st **(see Joining With Dc, page 17)**; tr in next 9 slip sts, 2 dc in next slip st, leave remaining sts unworked: 12 sts.

Row 2: Ch 3, turn; dc in same st and in next dc, tr in next 9 tr, dc in last dc; finish off: 13 sts.

SECOND WING
Row 1: With **right** side facing and working in free loops of slip sts on Rnd 1, skip one slip st from First Wing and join Red with dc in next slip st; dc in same st, tr in next 9 slip sts, dc in next slip st, leave remaining slip st unworked: 12 sts.

Row 2: Ch 3, turn; tr in next 9 tr, dc in next dc, 2 dc in last dc; finish off: 13 sts.

BACKGROUND
Rnd 1: With **right** side facing and working in sts on Rnd 3 of Lady Bug Body, join White with dc in second-to-the-last dc made; (2 dc in next dc, dc in next dc) 4 times, working in Back Loop Only of sts on Wing **and** in **both** loops of sts on Rnd 3, 2 dc in next st, dc in next st, 2 dc in next st, dc in next 6 sts, (2 dc in next st, dc in next st) twice, working in sts on Rnd 3 Only, 2 dc in next dc, (dc in next dc, 2 dc in next dc) 3 times, working in Back Loop Only of sts on Wing **and** in **both** loops of sts on Rnd 3, (dc in next st, 2 dc in next st) twice, dc in next 6 sts, 2 dc in next st, dc in next st, 2 dc in last st; join with slip st to first dc: 58 dc.

Rnd 2: Ch 3, dc in same st, (dc in next 2 dc, 2 dc in next dc) 5 times, dc in next 10 dc, 2 dc in next dc, (dc in next 2 dc, 2 dc in next dc) 6 times, dc in next 10 dc, 2 dc in next dc, dc in last 2 dc; join with slip st to first dc: 72 dc.

Rnd 3: Ch 1, sc in same st, ch 4, skip next 2 dc, ★ sc in next dc, ch 4, skip next 2 dc; repeat from ★ around; join with slip st to first sc, finish off: 24 ch-4 sps.

Rnd 4: With **right** side facing, join Green with slip st in first ch-4 sp; ch 4, work 2-dtr Cluster in same sp, ch 2, (work 3-dtr Cluster, ch 2) twice in same sp, † work 3-dtr Cluster in next ch-4 sp, ch 2, (work tr Cluster in next ch-4 sp, ch 2) twice, work 3-dtr Cluster in next ch-4 sp, ch 2, (work 3-dtr Cluster, ch 2) 3 times in next ch-4 sp, work 3-dtr Cluster in next ch-4 sp, ch 2, (work tr Cluster in next ch-4 sp, ch 2) 4 times, work 3-dtr Cluster in next ch-4 sp, ch 2 †, (work 3-dtr Cluster, ch 2) 3 times in next ch-4 sp, repeat from † to † once; join with slip st to top of first 2-dtr Cluster, finish off: 32 ch-2 sps.

Rnd 5: With **right** side facing, join White with dc in center 3-dtr Cluster of last corner made; 4 dc in same st, 3 dc in each ch-2 sp around working 5 dc in center 3-dtr Cluster of each corner; join with slip st to first dc, finish off: 116 dc.

BLOCK B (Make 10)
Work same as Block A through Rnd 5 of Background; do **not** finish off: 116 dc.

Begin working in rows.

Row 1: Slip st in next 2 dc, ch 4 **(counts as first dc plus ch 1, now and throughout)**, skip next 2 dc, 3 dc in sp **before** next dc **(Fig. 7, page 17)**, (skip next 3 dc, 3 dc in sp **before** next dc) 9 times, ch 1, skip next 2 dc, dc in next dc, leave remaining dc unworked: 32 dc and 2 ch-1 sps.

Row 2: Ch 3, turn; 2 dc in first ch-1 sp, skip next 3 dc, (3 dc in sp **before** next dc, skip next 3 dc) across to last ch-1 sp, 3 dc in last ch-1 sp: 33 dc.

Row 3: Ch 4, turn; skip next 2 dc, 3 dc in sp **before** next dc, (skip next 3 dc, 3 dc in sp **before** next dc) across to last 3 dc, ch 1, skip next 2 dc, dc in last dc: 32 dc and 2 ch-1 sps.

Row 4: Ch 3, turn; 2 dc in first ch-1 sp, skip next 3 dc, (3 dc in sp **before** next dc, skip next 3 dc) across to last ch-1 sp, 3 dc in last ch-1 sp; finish off.

ASSEMBLY

Using Placement Diagram as a guide and White, whipstitch Blocks together **(Fig. 8, page 17)**, forming 5 horizontal strips of 4 Blocks each; then whipstitch strips together in same manner.

PLACEMENT DIAGRAM

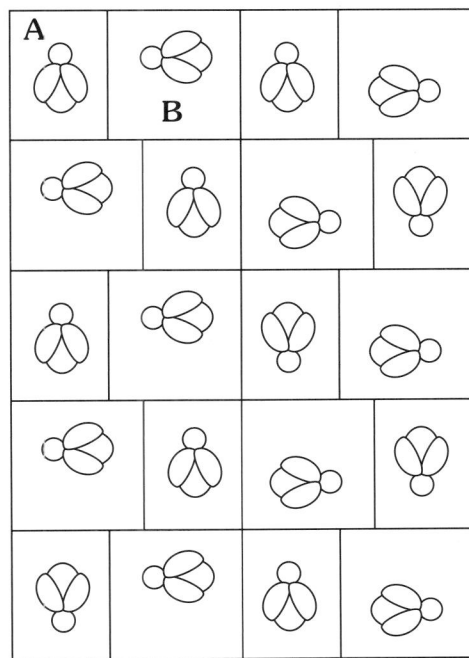

BORDER

Rnd 1: With **right** side facing and working across bottom of Afghan, join White with dc in center dc of corner 5-dc group; 2 dc in same st, working in sp **between** dc groups, 3 dc in each sp and in each seam across to next corner 5-dc group, skip next 2 dc, 5 dc in center dc, 3 dc in next 8 sps, working in end of rows, (3 dc in next row, skip next row) twice, ★ 3 dc in seam and in next 10 sps, 3 dc in seam and in next 8 sps, working in end of rows, (3 dc in next row, skip next row) twice; repeat from ★ once **more**, 5 dc in first dc on last row, 3 dc in each sp and in each seam across to next corner 5-dc group, skip next 2 dc, 5 dc in center dc, (3 dc in next 10 sps and in seam) 3 times, 3 dc in next 8 sps, working in end of rows, (3 dc in next row, skip next row) twice, 3 dc in seam and in last 10 sps, 2 dc in same st as first dc; join with slip st to first dc.

Rnd 2: Ch 3, 2 dc in same st, work Picot, working in sps **between** dc groups, (3 dc, work Picot) in each sp around working (3 dc, work Picot) in center dc of each corner 5-dc group; join with slip st to first dc, finish off.

FRENCH KNOT

Using photo as a guide for placement and two strands of Black, add French knots to Wings as follows:

Bring needle up at 1. Wrap yarn around the needle the desired number of times and insert needle at 2, holding end of yarn with non-stitching fingers **(Fig. 2)**. Tighten knot; then pull needle through, holding yarn until it must be released.

Fig. 2

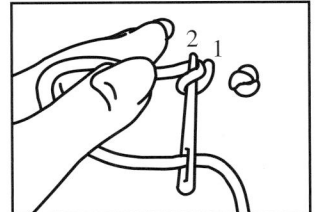

BUMBLE BEES AFGHAN

■■■□ INTERMEDIATE

Finished Size: 45" x 63" (114.5 cm x 160 cm)

MATERIALS
Medium/Worsted Weight Yarn (4)
[6 ounces, 326 yards
(170 grams, 298 meters) per skein]:
   Red - 5 skeins
   White - 1 skein
   Black - 1 skein
[5 ounces, 302 yards
(140 grams, 276 meters) per skein]:
   Yellow - 1 skein
Crochet hook, size H (5 mm) **or** size needed for gauge

GAUGE: Block A = 9"w x 12"h
   (22.75 cm x 30.5 cm);
   Block B = 12" (30.5 cm) square
   13 dc = 4" (10 cm)

Gauge Swatch: 6¼"w x 9¼"h
   (16 cm x 23.5 cm)
Work same as Block A through Background Rnd 4.

CHANGING COLORS
Insert hook in st indicated, YO and pull up a loop, drop yarn, with new yarn, YO and draw through both loops on hook *(Fig. 3)*. Carry yarn not being used along edge. Work over strands of yarn when working Rnd 1 of Background.

Fig. 3

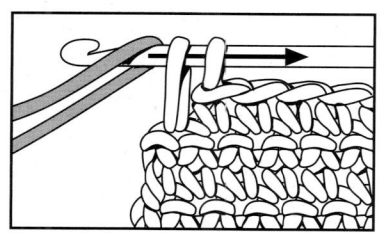

STITCH GUIDE
TREBLE CROCHET *(abbreviated tr)*
YO twice, insert hook in st indicated, YO and pull up a loop (4 loops on hook), (YO and draw through 2 loops on hook) 3 times.
DECREASE
Pull up a loop in next 2 sts, YO and draw through all 3 loops on hook **(counts as one sc)**.
PICOT
Ch 3, slip st in third ch from hook.

BLOCK A (Make 10)
BUMBLE BEE BODY
Row 1 (Right side)**:** With Black, ch 3, sc in second ch from hook and in last ch: 2 sc.

Note: Loop a short piece of yarn around any stitch to mark Row 1 as **right** side.

Row 2: Ch 1, turn; sc in first sc, 2 sc in last sc changing to Yellow in last sc made *(Fig. 3)*: 3 sc.

Row 3: Ch 1, turn; sc in each sc across.

Row 4: Ch 1, turn; sc in first sc, 2 sc in next sc, sc in last sc changing to Black: 4 sc.

Row 5: Ch 1, turn; sc in each sc across.

Row 6: Ch 1, turn; sc in first 2 sc, 2 sc in next sc, sc in last sc changing to Yellow: 5 sc.

Rows 7 and 8: Ch 1, turn; sc in each sc across; at end of Row 8, change to Black in last sc made.

Row 9: Ch 1, turn; sc in each sc across.

Row 10: Ch 1, turn; sc in first sc, decrease, sc in last 2 sc changing to Yellow in last sc made: 4 sc.

Instructions continued on page 11.

Row 11: Ch 1, turn; sc in each sc across.

Row 12: Ch 1, turn; sc in first sc, decrease, sc in last sc changing to Black, cut Yellow: 3 sc.

Row 13: Ch 1, turn; sc in each sc across.

Row 14: Ch 1, turn; sc in first sc, 2 sc in next sc, sc in last sc: 4 sc.

Row 15: Ch 1, turn; sc in first sc, 2 sc in next sc, sc in last 2 sc: 5 sc.

Row 16: Ch 1, turn; sc in first sc, decrease, sc in last 2 sc: 4 sc.

Row 17: Ch 1, turn; sc in first sc, decrease, sc in last sc: 3 sc.

Trim: Ch 1, do **not** turn; working in end of rows, sc in first 6 rows, place marker in last sc made for Wing placement, sc in each row across; working in free loops of beginning ch *(Fig. 5b, page 17)*, sc in first 2 chs; working in end of rows, sc in first 10 rows, place marker in last sc made for Wing placement, sc in each row across to last row, skip last row; sc in each sc across Row 17; join with slip st to first sc, finish off: 38 sc.

WINGS

First Pair: With **right** side facing, join White with slip st in Front Loop Only of first marked sc on Body Trim *(Fig. 4, page 17)*; remove marker, ch 12, tr in fifth ch from hook and in next 4 chs, dc in next ch, hdc in next ch, sc in last ch, slip st in Front Loop Only of next sc on Body Trim; ch 11, tr in fifth ch from hook and in next 3 chs, dc in next ch, hdc in next ch, sc in last ch, slip st in Front Loop Only of next sc on Body Trim; finish off.

Second Pair: With **right** side facing, join White with slip st in Front Loop Only of remaining marked sc; remove marker, ch 11, tr in fifth ch from hook and in next 3 chs, dc in next ch, hdc in next ch, sc in last ch, slip st in Front Loop Only of next sc on Body Trim; ch 12, tr in fifth ch from hook and in next 4 chs, dc in next ch, hdc in next ch, sc in last ch, slip st in Front Loop Only of next sc on Body Trim; finish off.

BACKGROUND

Rnd 1: With **right** side facing, join Red with dc in same st as joining on Body Trim *(see Joining With Dc, page 17)*; dc in next 3 sc, working **around** next sc *(Fig. 6, page 17)*, dc in same row **below**, working **behind** Wings, dc in free loop of next 3 sc on Body Trim *(Fig. 5a, page 17)*, working in **both** loops, hdc in next 3 sc, dc in next 5 sc, (dc, ch 3, dc) in next sc, dc in next 2 sc, (dc, ch 3, dc) in next sc, dc in next 5 sc, hdc in next 3 sc, working **behind** Wings, dc in free loop of next 3 sc, working **around** next sc, dc in same row **below**, working in **both** loops, dc in next 3 sc on Body Trim, (dc, ch 3, dc) in next sc, dc in last 2 sc and in same st as first dc, ch 1, hdc in first dc to form last ch-3 sp: 42 sts and 4 ch-3 sps.

Rnds 2-4: Ch 3 **(counts as first dc, now and throughout)**, dc in last ch-3 sp made and in each st around working (2 dc, ch 3, 2 dc) in each corner ch-3 sp, 2 dc in same sp as first dc, ch 1, hdc in first dc to form last ch-3 sp: 90 dc and 4 ch-3 sps.

Rnd 5: Ch 6 **(counts as first dc plus ch 3, now and throughout)**, dc in last ch-3 sp made, skip next 2 dc, (dc, ch 3, dc) in next dc, skip next 3 dc, † working in ch at tip of next Wing **and** in next dc, (dc, ch 3, dc) in next dc, [skip next 3 dc, (dc, ch 3, dc) in next dc] twice, skip next 3 dc, working in ch at tip of next Wing **and** in next dc, (dc, ch 3, dc) in next dc †, [skip next 3 dc, (dc, ch 3, dc) in next dc] twice, skip next 2 dc, dc in next corner ch-3 sp, (ch 3, dc in same sp) 3 times, skip next 2 dc, (dc, ch 3, dc) in next dc, [skip next 3 dc, (dc, ch 3, dc) in next dc] 3 times, skip next dc, dc in next corner ch-3 sp, (ch 3, dc in same sp) 3 times, skip next 2 dc, [(dc, ch 3, dc) in next dc, skip next 3 dc] twice, repeat from † to † once, skip next 3 dc, (dc, ch 3, dc) in next dc, skip next 2 dc, dc in next corner ch-3 sp, (ch 3, dc in same sp) 3 times, skip next 2 dc, (dc, ch 3, dc) in next dc, [skip next 3 dc, (dc, ch 3, dc) in next dc] 3 times, skip last dc, (dc, ch 3, dc) in same sp as first dc, ch 1, hdc in first dc to form last ch-3 sp: 34 ch-3 sps.

Rnd 6: Ch 6, dc in last ch-3 sp made, ★ (dc, ch 3, dc) in next ch-3 sp and in each ch-3 sp across to next corner ch-3 sp, dc in corner ch-3 sp, (ch 3, dc in same sp) 3 times; repeat from ★ 2 times **more**, (dc, ch 3, dc) in each ch-3 sp across and in same sp as first dc, ch 1, hdc in first dc to form last ch-3 sp; finish off: 42 ch-3 sps.

BLOCK B (Make 10)
Work same as Block A through Rnd 6 of Background; do **not** finish off: 42 ch-3 sps.

Begin working in rows.

Row 1: Ch 3, (dc, ch 3, dc) in next 11 ch-3 sps, dc in next ch-3 sp, leave remaining sps unworked: 11 ch-3 sps.

Rows 2-4: Ch 3, turn; (dc, ch 3, dc) in each ch-3 sp across, skip next dc, dc in last dc.

Finish off.

ASSEMBLY
Using Placement Diagram as guide, join Blocks together as follows:

With **right** sides of two Blocks facing, join Red with sc in corner sp on **first Block** *(see Joining With Sc, page 17)*, ch 1, sc in corner sp on **second Block**, ★ ch 1, sc in next sp on **first Block**, ch 1, sc in next sp on **second Block**; repeat from ★ across.

Join strips together in same manner.

PLACEMENT DIAGRAM

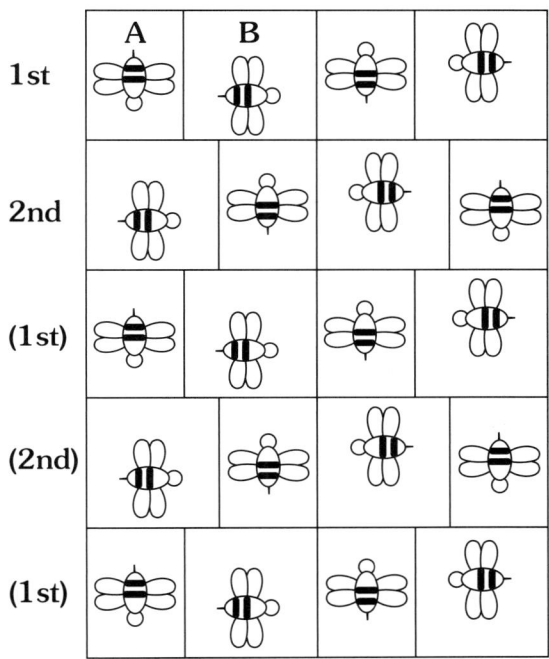

BORDER
With **right** side facing, join Red with dc in any corner ch-3 sp; work Picot, dc in same sp, (dc, work Picot, dc) in each sp around; join with slip st to first dc, finish off.

BUTTERFLIES AFGHAN

■■■□ INTERMEDIATE
Shown on Back Cover.

Finished Size: 39" x 51" (99 cm x 129.5 cm)

MATERIALS
Medium/Worsted Weight Yarn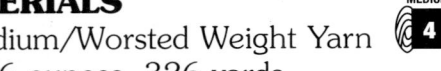
 [6 ounces, 326 yards
 (170 grams, 298 meters) per skein]:
  Black - 5 skeins
 [4 ounces, 242 yards
 (110 grams, 221 meters) per skein]:
  Variegated - 2 skeins
 [5 ounces, 302 yards
 (140 grams, 276 meters) per skein]:
  Pink - 1 skein
  Green - 1 skein
  Yellow - 1 skein
Crochet hook, size H (5 mm) **or** size needed for gauge

GAUGE: Each Block = 11" (28 cm) square
  13 dc = 4" (10 cm)

Gauge Swatch: 8½" (21.5 cm) square
Work same as Block through Background Rnd 6.

BLOCK (Make 12)
Referring to the table below, make the number of Blocks specified in the colors indicated.

	Block A Make 3	Block B Make 3	Block C Make 2	Block D Make 2	Block E Make 1	Block F Make 1
Body	Pink	Yellow	Green	Pink	Green	Yellow
Wings	Green	Pink	Yellow	Yellow	Pink	Green

BUTTERFLY BODY
With color indicated, ch 17.

Rnd 1 (Right side): (Dc, ch 2, slip st) in fourth ch from hook **(3 skipped chs count as first dc)**, sc in next ch and in each ch across, ch 1, place marker in ch just made for st placement; working in free loops on opposite side of beginning ch **(Fig. 5b, page 17)**, sc in first 3 chs, place marker around last sc made for Wing placement and to mark Body as **right** side, sc in next 10 chs, slip st in next ch, ch 2; join with slip st to first dc, finish off: 30 sts and 5 chs.

FIRST WING
Row 1: With **right** side facing and working in Front Loops Only **(Fig. 4, page 17)**, join color indicated with dc in first sc made **(see Joining With Dc, page 17)**; dc in same st and in next 3 sc, sc in next sc, working **around** next sc **(Fig. 6, page 17)**, sc in beginning ch, working in Front Loops Only, sc in next sc, dc in next 3 sc, 2 dc in next sc, leave remaining sts unworked: 13 sts.

Row 2: Ch 3 **(counts as first dc, now and throughout)**, turn; working in both loops, dc in same st and in next 4 dc, sc in next sc, slip st in next sc, sc in next sc, dc in next 4 dc, 2 dc in last dc: 15 sts.

13

Row 3: Ch 3, turn; dc in same st and in next 5 dc, sc in next sc, slip st in next slip st, sc in next sc, dc in next 5 dc, 2 dc in last dc: 17 sts.

Row 4: Ch 3, turn; dc in same st and in next 6 dc, sc in next sc, slip st in next slip st, sc in next sc, dc in next 6 dc, 2 dc in last dc; finish off: 19 sts.

SECOND WING
Row 1: With **right** side facing and working in Front Loops Only, join color indicated with dc in marked sc (do not remove marker); dc in same st and in next 3 sc, sc in next sc, working **around** next sc, sc in beginning ch, sc in next sc, dc in next 3 sc, 2 dc in next sc, leave remaining sts unworked: 13 sts.

Rows 2-4: Work same as First Wing.

BACKGROUND
Rnd 1: With **right** side facing, join Black with sc around marked ch on Body *(see Joining With Sc, page 17)*; remove marker, (sc, ch 3, dc) in next sc, dc in next sc, working **behind** Wing and in free loops of sc on Body *(Fig. 5a, page 17)*, dc in next 10 sc, working **around** next slip st, dc in beginning ch, dc in next ch, (dc, ch 3, sc) in next ch, skip next dc, working in **both** loops, sc in next dc, (sc, ch 3, dc) in next ch, dc in next ch, working **around** next slip st, dc in beginning ch, working **behind** Wing and in free loops of sc on Body, dc in next 10 sc, working in **both** loops, dc in next sc, (dc, ch 3, sc) in last sc; join with slip st to first sc: 36 sts and 4 ch-3 sps.

Rnd 2: Ch 1, sc in same st and in next sc, † (2 sc, ch 3, dc) in next ch-3 sp, dc in each dc across to next ch-3 sp, (dc, ch 3, 2 sc) in ch-3 sp †, sc in next 3 sc, repeat from † to † once, sc in last sc; join with slip st to first sc: 48 sts and 4 ch-3 sps.

Rnds 3 and 4: Ch 1, sc in same st and in each sc across to next corner ch-3 sp, † (2 sc, ch 3, dc) in corner ch-3 sp, dc in each dc across to next corner ch-3 sp, (dc, ch 3, 2 sc) in corner ch-3 sp †, sc in each sc across to next corner ch-3 sp, repeat from † to † once, sc in each sc across; join with slip st to first sc: 72 sts and 4 ch-3 sps.

Rnd 5: Ch 1, sc in same st and in next 7 sc, (2 sc, ch 3, dc) in next corner ch-3 sp, dc in next dc, working in first dc on Wing **and** in next dc, dc in next dc, † dc in next 17 dc, working in last dc on same Wing **and** in next dc, dc in next dc; dc in next dc, (dc, ch 3, 2 sc) in next corner ch-3 sp †, sc in next 15 sc, (2 sc, ch 3, dc) in next corner ch-3 sp, dc in next dc, working in first dc on next Wing **and** in next dc, dc in next dc, repeat from † to † once, sc in last 7 sc; join with slip st to first sc: 84 sts and 4 ch-3 sps.

Rnd 6: Repeat Rnd 3; finish off: 96 sts and 4 ch-3 sps.

Rnd 7: With **right** side facing and working across sc edge of Block, join Variegated with dc in corner ch-3 sp; (dc, ch 3, 2 dc) in same sp, † [skip next 2 sc, (2 dc, ch 2, 2 dc) in next sc, skip next 3 sc, (2 dc, ch 2, 2 dc) in next sc] 3 times, skip next 2 sc, (2 dc, ch 3, 2 dc) in next corner ch-3 sp, skip next 2 dc, (2 dc, ch 2, 2 dc) in next dc, [skip next 3 dc, (2 dc, ch 2, 2 dc) in next dc] 5 times, skip next 2 dc †, (2 dc, ch 3, 2 dc) in next ch-3 sp, repeat from † to † once; join with slip st to first dc, finish off: 28 sps.

Rnd 8: With **right** side facing, join Black with dc in any corner ch-3 sp; (3 dc, ch 1, 4 dc) in same sp, 4 dc in each ch-2 sp around working (4 dc, ch 1, 4 dc) in each corner ch-3 sp; join with slip st to first dc, finish off: 32 4-dc groups and 4 ch-1 sps.

ASSEMBLY

Using Placement Diagram as a guide, join Blocks together as follows:

With **right** side of two Blocks facing, join Black with sc in corner ch-1 sp on **first Block**; ch 3, sc in corresponding corner ch-1 sp on **second Block**, ch 3, ★ skip next 4 dc on **first Block**, sc in sp **before** next dc *(Fig. 7, page 17)*, ch 3, skip next 4 dc on **second Block**, sc in sp **before** next dc, ch 3; repeat from ★ 6 times **more**, skip next 4 dc on **first Block**, sc in next corner ch-1 sp, ch 3, skip next 4 dc on **second Block**, sc in next corner ch-1 sp; finish off.

Join strips together in same manner.

PLACEMENT DIAGRAM

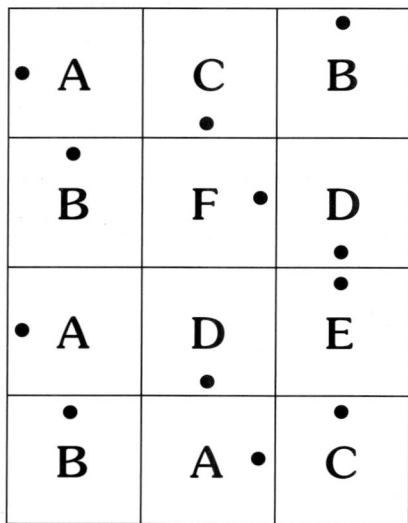

BORDER

Rnd 1: With **right** side facing, join Black with sc in any corner ch-1 sp, working in sps **between** 4-dc groups and in corner ch-1 sps on each Block, (ch 5, sc in next sp) around, ch 2, dc in first sc to form last ch-5 sp.

Rnd 2: Ch 1, sc in last ch-5 sp made, ch 5, (sc in next ch-5 sp, ch 5) around; join with slip st to first sc.

Rnd 3: Slip st in first ch-5 sp, ch 3, (dc, ch 2, 2 dc) in same sp, (2 dc, ch 2, 2 dc) in next ch-5 sp and in each ch-5 sp around; join with slip st to first dc, finish off.

Rnd 4: With **right** side facing, join Variegated with dc in any corner ch-2 sp; **[**dc, (ch 2, 2 dc) twice**]** in same sp, (2 dc, ch 2, 2 dc) in next ch-2 sp and in each ch-2 sp across to next corner ch-2 sp, ★ 2 dc in corner ch-2 sp, (ch 2, 2 dc in same sp) twice, (2 dc, ch 2, 2 dc) in next ch-2 sp and in each ch-2 sp across to next corner ch-2 sp; repeat from ★ 2 times **more**; join with slip st to first dc, finish off.

GENERAL INSTRUCTIONS

ABBREVIATIONS

ch(s)   chain(s)
cm   centimeters
dc   double crochet(s)
dtr   double treble crochet(s)
hdc   half double crochet(s)
mm   millimeters
Rnd(s) Round(s)
sc   single crochet(s)
sp(s)   space(s)
st(s)   stitch(es)
tr   treble crochet(s)
YO   yarn over

★ — work instructions following ★ as many **more** times as indicated in addition to the first time.

† to † or ♥ to ♥ — work all instructions from first † to second † or from first ♥ to second ♥ **as many** times as specified.

( ) or [ ] — work enclosed instructions **as many** times as specified by the number immediately following **or** work all enclosed instructions in the stitch or space indicated **or** contains explanatory remarks.

colon (:) — the number(s) given after a colon at the end of a row or round denote(s) the number of stitches or spaces you should have on that row or round.

GAUGE

Exact gauge is **essential** for proper size. Before beginning your afghan, make the sample swatch given in the individual instructions in the yarn and hook specified. After completing the swatch, measure it, counting your stitches and rows carefully. If your swatch is larger or smaller than specified, **make another, changing hook size to get the correct gauge**. Keep trying until you find the size hook that will give you the specified gauge.

CROCHET TERMINOLOGY	
UNITED STATES	INTERNATIONAL
slip stitch (slip st) =	single crochet (sc)
single crochet (sc) =	double crochet (dc)
half double crochet (hdc) =	half treble crochet (htr)
double crochet (dc) =	treble crochet (tr)
treble crochet (tr) =	double treble crochet (dtr)
double treble crochet (dtr) =	triple treble crochet (ttr)
triple treble crochet (tr tr) =	quadruple treble crochet (qtr)
skip =	miss

Yarn Weight Symbol & Names	SUPER FINE 1	FINE 2	LIGHT 3	MEDIUM 4	BULKY 5	SUPER BULKY 6
Type of Yarns in Category	Sock, Fingering Baby	Sport, Baby	DK, Light Worsted	Worsted, Afghan, Aran	Chunky, Craft, Rug	Bulky, Roving
Crochet Gauge Ranges in Single Crochet to 4" (10 cm)	21-32 sts	16-20 sts	12-17 sts	11-14 sts	8-11 sts	5-9 sts
Advised Hook Size Range	B-1 to E-4	E-4 to 7	7 to I-9	I-9 to K-10.5	K-10.5 to M-13	M-13 and larger

ALUMINUM CROCHET HOOKS												
U.S.	B-1	C-2	D-3	E-4	F-5	G-6	H-8	I-9	J-10	K-10½	N	P	Q
Metric - mm	2.25	2.75	3.25	3.5	3.75	4	5	5.5	6	6.5	9	10	15

■□□□ BEGINNER	Projects for first-time crocheters using basic stitches. Minimal shaping.
■■□□ EASY	Projects using yarn with basic stitches, repetitive stitch patterns, simple color changes, and simple shaping and finishing.
■■■□ INTERMEDIATE	Projects using a variety of techniques, such as basic lace patterns or color patterns, mid-level shaping and finishing.
■■■■ EXPERIENCED	Projects with intricate stitch patterns, techniques and dimension, such as non-repeating patterns, multi-color techniques, fine threads, small hooks, detailed shaping and refined finishing.

JOINING WITH SC

When instructed to join with sc, begin with a slip knot on hook. Insert hook in stitch or space indicated, YO and pull up a loop, YO and draw through both loops on hook.

JOINING WITH DC

When instructed to join with dc, begin with a slip knot on hook. YO, holding loop on hook, insert hook in stitch or space indicated, YO and pull up a loop (3 loops on hook), (YO and draw through 2 loops on hook) twice.

BACK OR FRONT LOOP ONLY

Work only in loop(s) indicated by arrow **(Fig. 4)**.

Fig. 4

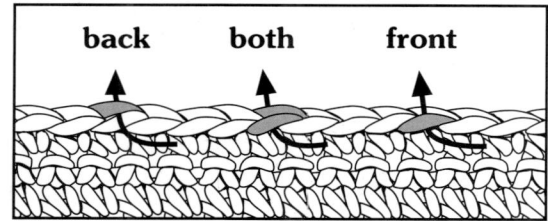

FREE LOOPS

After working in Back or Front Loops Only on a row or round, there will be a ridge of unused loops. These are called the free loops. Later, when instructed to work in the free loops of the same row or round, work in these loops **(Fig. 5a)**.

When instructed to work in free loops of a chain, work in loop indicated by arrow **(Fig. 5b)**.

Fig. 5a

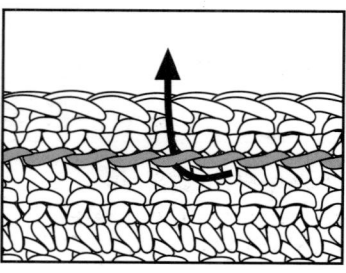

Fig. 5b

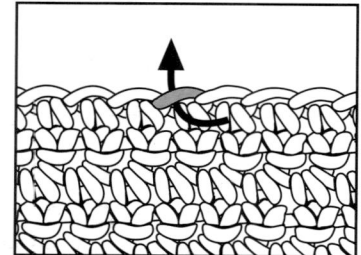

WORKING AROUND A STITCH

Work in stitch or space indicated, inserting hook in direction of arrow **(Fig. 6)**.

Fig. 6

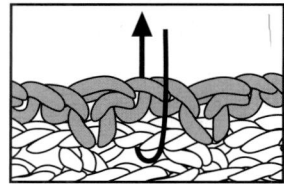

WORKING IN SPACE BEFORE A STITCH

When instructed to work in space **before** a stitch or in spaces **between** stitches, insert hook in space indicated by arrow **(Fig. 7)**.

Fig. 7

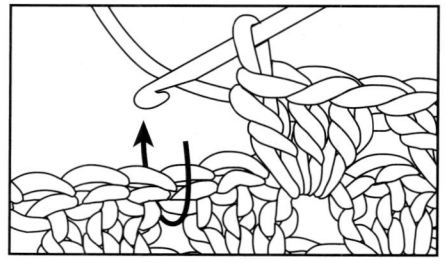

WHIPSTITCH

Place two Blocks with **wrong** sides together. Beginning in corner, sew through both pieces once to secure the beginning of the seam, leaving an ample yarn end to weave in later. Working through **both** loops of each stitch on **both** pieces, insert the needle from front to back through first stitch and pull yarn through **(Fig. 8)**, ★ insert the needle from front to back through next stitch and pull yarn through; repeat from ★ across.

Fig. 8

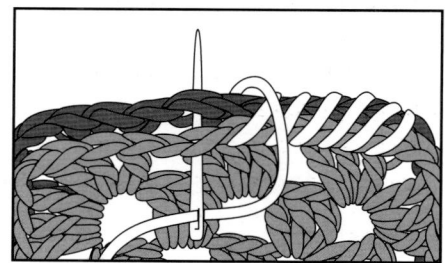